#71
Westwood Branch
1246 Glendon Ave.
Los Angeles, CA 90024

Native Americans

California Indians

Mir Tamim Ansary

Heinemann Library
Chicago, Illinois

Customer Service 888-454-2279

Printed in Hong Kong
Designed by Depke Design

04 03 02 01
10 9 8 7 6 5 4 3

Library of Congress Cataloging-in-Publication Data
Ansary, Mir Tamim.
    California Indians / Mir Tamim Ansary.
      p. cm. – (Native Americans)
    Includes bibliographical references and index.
    Summary: Describes the traditional way of life of the Indians of
California and the changes brought to it by Europeans, discussing
homes, clothing, games, crafts, and beliefs.
    ISBN 1-57572-927-X (library binding)
    1. Indians of North American-California Juvenile literature.
[1. Indians of North America-California.] I Title. II. Series:
Ansary, Mir Tamim. Native Americans.
E78.C15A677 2000
979.4004'97-dc21
                                         99-37136
                                          CIP

Acknowledgments
The author and publishers are grateful to the following for permission to reproduce copyright material:
Cover: Ben Klaffke
AP/Wide World Photos, p. 30 top; Mark Bolster, p. 22; Edward S. Curtis/National Geographic Image Collection, pp. 9,
10, 12, 20; D-Q University, p. 28; Dr. D.E. Degginger, p. 5; Phil Degginger, p. 24; Trudy Haversat/Gary S. Breschini, p. 23;
Ben Klaffke, pp. 4, 8, 13, 18; National Anthropological Archives, pp. 7, 21; North Wind Pictures, pp. 11, 25; Peabody
Museum/Harvard University, p. 15; Phoebe Hearst Museum of Anthropology, University of California at Berkeley, pp.
27, 30 bottom; Santa Barbara Historical Society, p. 14; Stock Montage, Inc., p. 26; Mickey Vallo/Courtesy Trees
Company, p. 29; Marilyn Angel Wynn, pp. 16, 17, 19.

Every effort has been made to contact copyright holders of any material reproduced in this book. Any omissions will be
rectified in subsequent printings if notice is given to the publisher.

Our special thanks to Lana Grant, Native American MLS, for her
help in the preparation of this book.

Note to the Reader Some words are shown in bold, **like this.** You can find
out what they mean by looking in the glossary.

Contents

A World Apart 4
Land of Plenty 6
A Rich Diet 8
Houses of Many Styles 10
Dressing Simple, Dressing Fancy 12
Group Life 14
Trade and Wealth 16
Arts and Crafts 18
Becoming an Adult 20
Sacred Places 22
The Mission Era 24
After the Gold Rush 26
The 20th Century 28
Famous California Indians 30
Glossary 31
More Books to Read 32
Index 32

A World Apart

California is a region surrounded by natural barriers. The Sierra Nevada mountains wall it off in the east. The Siskiyou Mountains rise in the north. To the west of California lies the Pacific Ocean. The Mojave Desert is in the south.

Within these **borders** are many small worlds. There are places in California where the snow never melts. There are places where the sun shines almost every day. California has rain-soaked valleys and sun-baked deserts. It has beaches, bays, grasslands, forests, and much more.

PACIFIC
OCEAN

NORTH
AMERICA

ATLANTIC
OCEAN

CALIFORNIA

N

Areas where
California
Indians live

500 miles
800 kilometers

Land of Plenty

People moved into California in small groups over thousands of years. These people hunted animals and gathered plants for food. Before moving to California, they roamed all the time. They could not stay in one place because they would use up all the food. California, however, was a land of plenty.

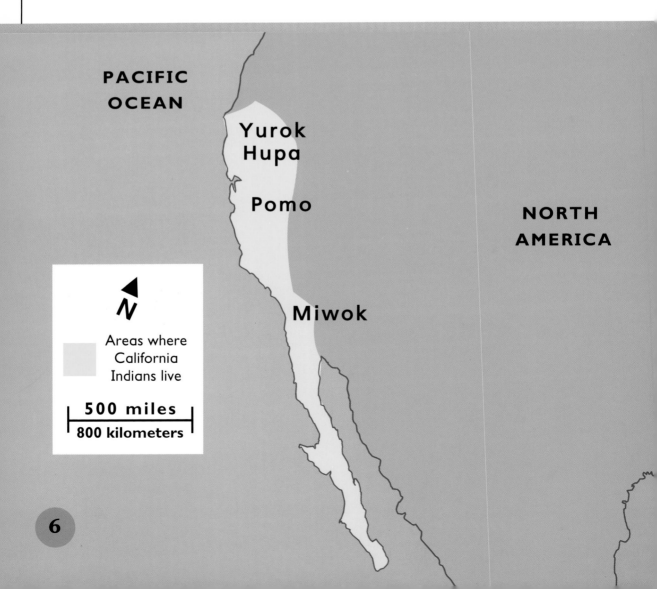

PACIFIC OCEAN

Yurok
Hupa

Pomo

NORTH AMERICA

Miwok

N

Areas where California Indians live

500 miles
800 kilometers

In California, people could get all they needed in one small area. Therefore, each group of hunters and gatherers settled someplace. By 1500, California was like a **patchwork** of little countries. More than 350 thousand people lived here. They were divided into hundreds of groups, speaking many languages. Each group had its own territory.

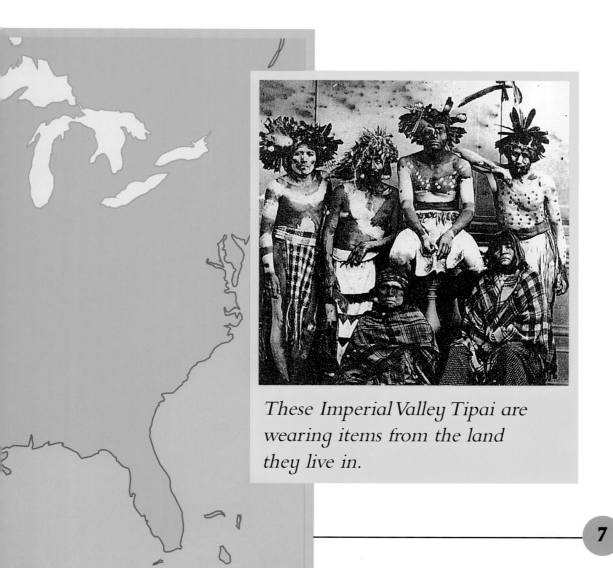

These Imperial Valley Tipai are wearing items from the land they live in.

A Rich Diet

In those days, California had many oak trees, which have nuts called acorns. Acorns became the most important food of the California Indians. They took the place of corn and other grains. People who didn't have acorns got them through trade. Hardly anyone became a farmer.

California Indians made flour, porridge, and soup out of acorns.

Rivers and streams provided plenty of trout and other fish.

Besides acorns, people ate almost everything they could hunt, fish, or gather. They ate wild fruits, cactuses, bulrushes—a tall plant, and roots. Salmon, elk, and rabbits were also popular. **Abalone**, earthworms, grasshoppers, and turtles all were eaten by some group in California.

Houses of Many Styles

A traveler in old California would have seen many types of houses. The Yurok people made square houses out of planks of wood. The Miwok made cone-shaped shelters out of bark. Clay, brush, and reeds were used in various places. Roofs might be flat, slanted, or domed. Some houses were partly underground.

In Central California, people built brush shelters while traveling to gather food.

This village of cone-shaped houses was located in central California, near Yuba City.

In central California, each village had a roundhouse. Villagers used this big building for dances and gatherings. Most villages had a sweathouse, too, especially in the north. The men used the sweathouse every day. Often, all the men slept in the sweathouse. Women and children slept in the regular houses.

Dressing Simple, Dressing Fancy

Everyday clothing in California was simple. Women wore skirts of bark or twisted grass. In the rain, they wore basketlike hats. In cold weather, both men and women wore cloaks, or coats, made from the fur of otters or other animals. Children usually wore nothing.

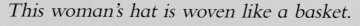
This woman's hat is woven like a basket.

These Hupa dancers are wearing headbands decorated with woodpecker feathers.

During warm weather, most men wore clothes only at special times. The Hupa people, for example, had a two-week festival called the Deer Dance. Men dressed up for this important event. They wore robes of rare white deerskin. They wore colorful **headdresses** made from the feathers of such birds as the red woodpecker.

Group Life

In California, few groups were big enough to be called tribes. Most groups were made up of a few related families who lived near each other. These groups did not have real chiefs. A rich man was usually respected, but he could not make laws. He gave people advice, but he could not give them orders.

This drawing by Russell Ruiz shows daily life in a Chumash village.

A Karuk shaman in Northern California would wear this hat to perform a healing dance for a sick child.

Some people called *shamans* were respected because they had powerful dreams. In the north, most shamans were women. People looked to them as healers, but not as rulers. There was little need for rulers, lawmakers, or chiefs in California. Rarely did one group attack another. There were no armies. War was almost unknown here.

Trade and Wealth

If people wanted something they didn't have, they traded for it. Acorns, wood, furs, and special stones, such as **flint** and **obsidian,** were among the goods people traded. A seashell called *dentalium* was used as money throughout most of California. A string of these shells was called *kaia*.

Dentalium shells like these were used as money in California.

16

Beads and shells like these were often used when trading.

Money was important in daily life. Young men needed *kaia* to get married. They paid the bride's parents. Someone who hurt another person had to pay that person. The Yurok people had **fines** for all kinds of bad behavior. The winner of a fight might end up poor, even though he won. This kept people from starting fights.

Arts and Crafts

Making baskets was the great art of the California Indians. It remains so today. Reeds and grasses of different colors are used to weave patterns. The Pomo Indians work shells, feathers, and beads into their baskets. Some Pomo baskets are so tiny that the stitches are hard to see.

The patterns woven into this Hupa basket come from stones, feathers, and reeds of different colors, all woven together.

Rattles, such as the split stick clapper in the middle, are important musical instruments in California.

Music is another great California art. In fact, no festival is complete without it. Dancers play double whistles. They shake rattles made from deer hooves. A drum is made by placing a large board over a pit in the ground. People play by dancing on the board. Split-stick clappers can make sounds like rattlesnakes or even thunder.

Becoming an Adult

Girls went through important **rituals** when they became adults. They lived alone. They kept their heads covered. They drank hot liquids and took many steam baths. Once these rituals ended, the girl was accepted as a woman. Then came a celebration that often lasted ten days or more.

Many tribes thought a teenage girl should not drink or bathe in cold water.

Becoming a man meant a boy could join in the religious ceremonies and dances of his group.

When boys became adults, they entered a religious **society**. In the north, for example, boys joined a Kuksu **cult**. Kuksu is the name of a powerful **spirit**. At a Kuksu **ceremony**, men sing and perform religious stories in which they play the parts of different spirits.

Sacred Places

California Indians had religious respect for the areas where they lived. They believed they had always lived in that place. Usually, they believed that one special spot within their area was **sacred**. Some myths say their **ancestors** rose out of the earth at this "place of power."

A rock, like this one in Yosemite National Park, was thought to be a scared place of great power.

These figures were painted by Salinan Indians in an area now called Monterey County.

In many of these sacred places, rock art can be found. Pictures and **symbols** have been carved into or painted onto the rocks. Much of this rock art is hundreds of years old, and yet the colors are still bright. California has more rock art than any other region in the United States.

The Mission Era

In 1769, a Spanish priest named Junipero Serra came to California. He built many churches along the coast. These churches were called missions. The Spanish captured Indians who lived near the missions. The Indians were forced to speak Spanish, study Christianity, and work for the mission.

This mission in Carmel was built in 1770 by the Spanish priest Father Junipero Serra.

Women and even children were put to work on Spanish missions.

Indians were not allowed to leave the missions. They were punished for speaking their own languages. These peaceful people knew nothing of war. They could not fight against the Spanish. Many died of illness or overwork. By 1848, only about 100 thousand Native Americans were left in California.

After the Gold Rush

In 1848, the United States took over California. That year, gold was found in the region. The **miners** who moved into California attacked the Indians, often just for fun. Whole tribes were wiped out. At last, in 1851, the U.S. government signed **treaties** with eighteen Native American groups of California.

Miners who came to California to find gold brought great suffering to the Native Americans of this region.

Ishi grew up in hiding until the rest of his family band had died. He came out of hiding in 1911.

These groups were promised more than seven million **acres** of **reservation** land. The promises were broken, however. California Indians got fewer than half a million acres in the end. And White settlers kept attacking them. By 1900, the number of Native Americans in California was down to 15,000.

The 20th Century

After 1900, life improved a little for California Indians. By 1970, the number of Indians had risen to 40,000. Today, there is a Native American college called D-Q University near the city of Sacramento. Here, the history of California Indians is being studied. The languages that have not been lost are being written down, taped, and videotaped.

Here, a Native American student sits by the front entrance to D-Q University.

*Many Native Americans today are learning and teaching the traditional crafts of their **ancestors.***

Festivals, such as the Deer Dance, are still celebrated. Old Indian communities are building new roundhouses. And Indians from many other areas of the United States have moved to California. They are meeting each other here and learning one another's ways. Out of the mixture, a new Native American culture may be rising in California.

Famous California Indians

Michael Dorris (Modoc, 1945–1997) taught Native American Studies at Dartmouth College. He also wrote novels, stories, and essays. His best-known book is *Yellow Raft in Blue Water. Crown of Columbus,* which he co-wrote with his wife Louise Erdrich, was published just before Dorris's death.

Ishi (Yahi, 1862–1916) Ishi grew up in hiding. In 1911, he came out of the woods because the rest of his band had died. He spent his last five years at the Museum of Anthropology in San Francisco. He learned English and taught others much about the Yahi way of life.

Keintpuash (Modoc, ?–1873) was known to Whites as "Captain Jack." In 1872 he refused an order to move onto a **reservation.** Instead, he and his followers fought the U.S. Army for months. The Modoc war ended with Keintpuash's capture in 1873.

Glossary

abalone type of shellfish

acre measure of land about the size of a soccer field

ancestor someone who comes early in a family's history

barrier something that blocks the way

border place where one area ends and another begins

ceremony set of acts that has special meaning, often for religious reasons

cult way of worshiping, usually having religious meaning

fine money paid as punishment

flint stone that sparks when hit with steel, used to make fire

headdress special hat

miner person who digs out minerals from the earth

obsidian black, glasslike stone used to make arrowheads

patchwork something made from many small parts

reservation area of land set aside for Native Americans

ritual set of acts, usually for religious reasons

sacred given great respect for religious reasons

society people living together as a group with the same way of life

spirit being that has life but cannot be seen, often having special powers

symbol object, picture, or sign that stands for something else, such as an idea

treaty written agreement between groups of people or countries that settles an argument

More Books to Read

Covert, Kim. *Miwok Indians.* Danbury, Conn.: Children's Press, 1998.

Lund, Bill. *The Pomo Indians.* Danbury, Conn.: Children's Press, 1997.

Rawls, James J. *Never Turn Back: Father Serra's Mission.* Austin, Tex.: Raintree Steck-Vaughn, 1992.

Index

baskets 10, 16, 18

Captain Jack 30
clothing 12, 13, 15

dances 11, 13, 15, 19, 21, 29

Dorris, Michael 30

farming 6
festivals 13, 19, 29
fish 9
food 4, 6, 8, 9, 10,

gatherings 11
Gold Rush 24

healers 15
houses 10, 11, 29
Hupa 6, 13, 18

Ishi 27, 30

kaia 14
Keintpuash 30
Kuksu 21

languages 7, 25, 28
laws 14, 15

miners 26
missions 24, 25
Miwok 6, 10
Modoc 30
Mojave Desert 4
money 16, 17
music 19, 21
myths 22

Pomo 6, 18

religion 21, 22, 23, 24
rock art 23

salmon 9
Serra, Father Junipero 24
settlers 27
shamans 15
Sierra Nevada 4
Siskiyou 4
Spanish 24, 25
sweathouse 11

trade 8, 16

war 15, 25, 30

Yahi 30
Yurok 6, 10, 17